INTRODUCTION

TO

MATLAB

for Beginners

Daniel Okoh and Eric Nwokolo

Preface

The MATLAB programming language has fast gained popularity among scientists, engineers, and in whole lot careers where immense computing is required. It has been described as the language of technical computing.

This book presents very basic introduction to MATLAB, especially for persons that have never seen or used the software before. To be very candid, we wrote this book for beginners who want to teach themselves how to start using MATLAB.

Table of Contents

Chapter 1

Introduction

This book is a perfect MATLAB tutor for anyone who has not used MATLAB before. In fact, the book is written with the assumption that the reader has never seen nor touched the MATLAB software before. So, if you have heard anything about MATLAB before now, just consider it an added advantage, but it doesn't stop us from presenting the ideas and activities as fundamental as possible. We will try to present everything as simple as possible so that anyone interested in learning

MATLAB can do so using the book with very little or no external assistance.

1.1 A bit of what MATLAB is and what it is not

Most persons that hear the word 'MATLAB' quickly think it is a tool/software for solving or doing Mathematics. This is not very true! While the MATLAB software is well-equipped for persons interested in solving mathematical problems, it is not just a tool for doing maths. Fact is that the 'MAT' in MATLAB doesn't stand for mathematics as often suggested or misconstrued. The 'MAT' in MATLAB stands for MATRIX, and the full meaning of MATLAB is MATRIX LABORATORY.

Why Matrix Laboratory? This is because MATLAB is designed with the primary intention of being able to carry out operations in 'bulk' or on so many objects at the same time, unlike is the case with several other programming languages. If you've heard of a matrix before, you'll probably have known it to mean a collection of so many items; usually numbers in the case of mathematics, but not restricted to numbers in the use of MATLAB. We'll see this shortly in the course of this learning.

MATLAB is also a high programming language, and NO! this doesn't suggest that MATLAB is difficult (or highly technical) to use, but on the contrary means that MATLAB is simpler/easier to learn and use when compared to most other programming languages. When a programming language is described as 'low', it somewhat mean that such a programming language is more difficult to learn/use. At the early years of computer development, computer programming was a thing reserved for the 'gurus' who could script things that made no sense to ordinary

humans, yes they used the low programming languages. Recently, attention is drifting to programming languages that have very close semblance to human languages so that they are easier to learn and use, these are called high programming languages, MATLAB falls in this category. Essentially, if you use a high programming language, you could achieve in one line, what it will have taken hundreds of lines to achieve in a low programming language! **So be happy and relaxed, what we want to do is really interesting!**

1.2 Starting/Launching the MATLAB Software

Since the assumption is that you've never seen nor used MATLAB before, we are going to begin by showing you where and how to open the MATLAB software.

First, you need to have installed MATLAB on your computer. This is definitely one thing you'll need someone to help you do, especially if you've never installed any software before. If however you've done this before, then you shouldn't have a problem installing the MATLAB software by yourself. For help on how to do this, visit the MATLAB website: www.mathworks.com

Once you have MATLAB installed on your computer, you usually will see an icon for it on the Desktop as illustrated below:

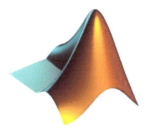

Figure 1: The MATLAB ICON

A fast and popular way to launch/start MATLAB is to double-click on this icon, and it will open the MATLAB environment as discussed in the next section.

1.3 Introduction to the MATLAB Environment

When opened for the first time, the MATLAB environment will look as illustrated below. Don't be bothered if yours doesn't look exactly! There may be very little difference, but in overall you'll notice the features discussed below.

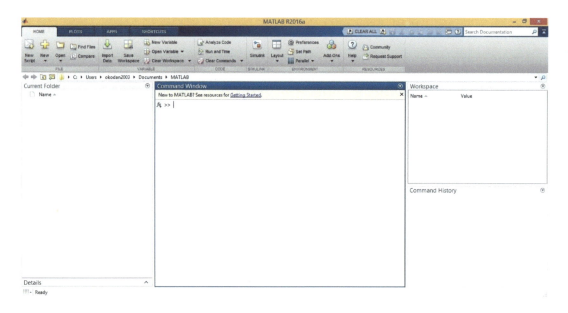

Figure 2: The MATLAB Environment

The main features we'll like you to take note of are explained below. We will briefly and quickly go through them here and expose you more to them later on.

1.3.1. The Command Window

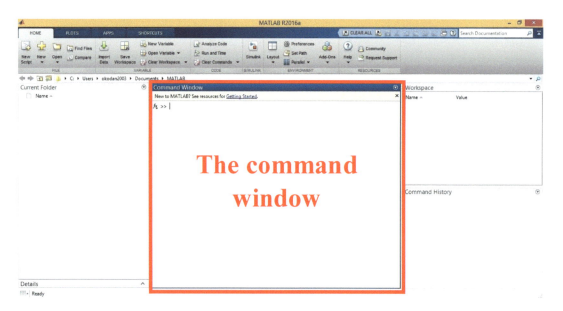

Figure 3: The Command Window on the MATLAB Environment

The command window is where MATLAB commands are 'run' and where results are usually displayed. It is the window you are most likely to be needing on MATLAB.

You type commands immediately after the prompt sign '>>' as on the top left hand corner of the command window. For a simple illustration, let's try to solve 5+3 on MATLAB; all you need to do is type '5+3' on the command window, and then press the 'Enter' key on your keyboard. The answer is displayed on the command window (see figure below).

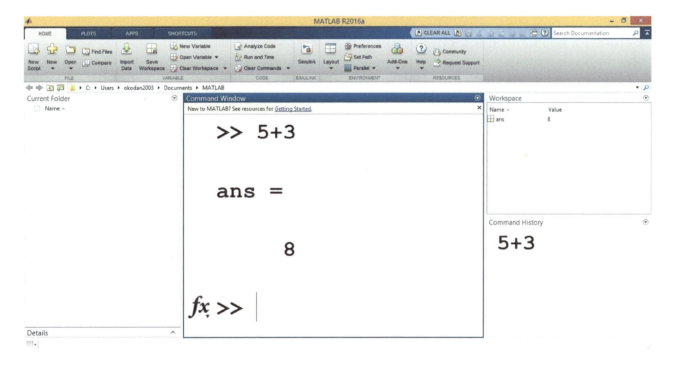

Figure 4: Illustrating how to run commands on the Command Window

1.3.2. The Command History

The command history is illustrated in Figure 5. It automatically saves all commands that are 'run' on the command window. For example, when we ran the command '5+3', the command history automatically saved it (see figure 4).

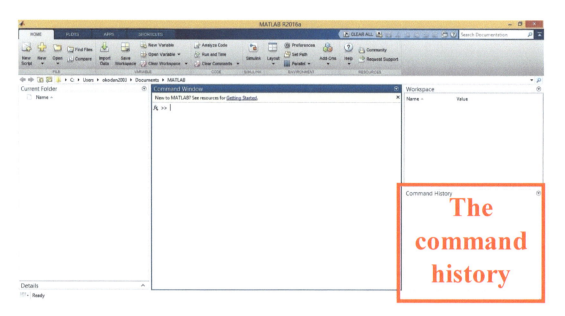

Figure 5: The Command History on the MATLAB Environment

The command history is useful in one way: you do not need to repeatedly type commands you have ran before on the command window. All you need to do is to double-click any of the commands on the command history and it will automatically run again on the command window.

Apart from saving you the stress of retyping commands you already ran on the command window, the command history also helps you save those commands in the order they were ran starting from the first to the last. So you can always verify the sequence you previously ran commands on the command window.

HINT: You can also get a history of commands you previously ran on the command window without necessarily going to the command history: While on the prompt '>>' of the command window, just press the up arrow key on your keyboard (this brings up the command you ran last on the command window), pressing the up arrow key again brings up the command before the last one,…. and so on.

1.3.3. The Workspace

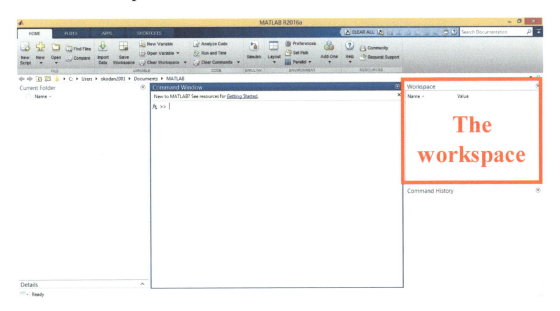

Figure 6: The Workspace on the MATLAB Environment

The workspace displays information on variables/parameters used in programs that are run on MATLAB. For example, when we ran the command '5+3', the answer (which is 8) is displayed as 'ans' (short form for answer) on the workspace. See Figure 4. We will learn more about the workspace as we work more on MATLAB.

Just For Your Information: 5+3 is usually not the kind of stuff we do on MATLAB! We use it here only for simple illustration purpose. You'll soon get to learn of very interesting and fascinating stuff you can do with MATLAB.

1.3.4. The Current Folder

You have to understand this! That each time you open or use the MATLAB software, there is a directory (or folder) on your computer you are working from. You can always check to see what folder it is at the top of the MATLAB software (see the arrow in figure 7). By default, it is usually the MATLAB folder on your computer, e.g.:

C:\Users\okodan2003\Documents\MATLAB

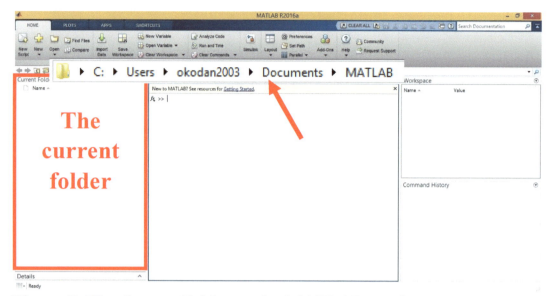

Figure 7: The Current Folder on the MATLAB Environment

You can always change this folder at your discretion, but this shouldn't be an issue now! Feel free to always work on whatever folder the software opens with. If there is need to change it, you'll certainly know. We'll talk more about how to change it in subsequent lessons.

1.3.5. The Editor and More

The Editor is another very important window on the MATLAB environment (not shown in our figures here), but will be treated extensively on our series on 'MATLAB Scripting & File Processing'. The editor is used for writing MATLAB scripts/programs that can be conveniently shared with other users.

There are also a couple of other features on the MATLAB environment you'll get to learn as we progress. So, let's go and get started.

Chapter 2

Building Matrices

Matrices are about the most useful tools in MATLAB; it is what has distinguished MATLAB programming and made it a lot easier and interesting than other conventional programming languages. This is why we think you should start here. In this chapter, we are going to see very interesting ways to generate/build matrices on MATLAB. You may not see how useful this will be to you at this stage, but believe me this is definitely something you'll find crucial when you become a MATLAB programmer! So, let's quickly do it.

2.1 Typing in Matrix Entries

One way of generating matrices on MATLAB is to type them in. This is usually the case if the size of the matrix is small, say a 3-by-2 matrix.

Suppose we want to type in a 3-by-2 matrix (let's call the matrix M) as shown below:

$$M = \begin{pmatrix} 4 & 7 \\ -3 & 1 \\ 0 & -2 \end{pmatrix}$$

All we need to do is type the entries into MATLAB as shown below, using the semicolon to indicate end of rows.

M=[4 7; -3 1; 0 -2]

When you press the 'Enter' key on your keyboard, MATLAB displays

the MATRIX in the correct order.

Observe the following:

1. The matrix elements are entered in square brackets. That is

[matrix elements here]

MATLAB understands square brackets to be used to collect entries/elements of matrices.

2. The semi-colon (that is, ;) is used to indicate the end of each line/row of the matrix.

3. Elements in the same row are separated with a space.

Good! Now can you attempt to say the size of matrix A typed as shown below:

A = [3 -2 4 5 -1; 8 19 -6 9 0; 4 5 6 7 20; 4 0 56 -70 9]

4-by-5? That's correct! If you type that on the MATLAB command window and press enter, you'll actually get the result shown below.

$$A = \begin{pmatrix} 3 & -2 & 4 & 5 & -1 \\ 8 & 19 & -6 & 9 & 0 \\ 4 & 5 & 6 & 7 & 20 \\ 4 & 0 & 56 & -70 & 9 \end{pmatrix}$$

HINT: You can also use a comma (,) to separate elements in the same row of a matrix.

2.2 Importing Data from External Files

If you already have a collection of data in an external file (e.g an excel or text file), you can import the data by clicking on the 'Import Data' icon as shown in Figure 8 below.

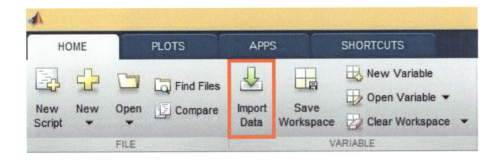

Figure 8: Importing Data

A dialog box pops up for you to choose the file where the data is stored. When you do this and Click **Open**, the Import Wizard opens the contents of the file allowing you to import the data into MATLAB.

Let's suppose we want to load data from the excel file illustrated in Figure 9.

First, we click on the **Import Data** icon. When the dialog box pops up, we browse to the file containing the data and select it. Then click the **Open** button.

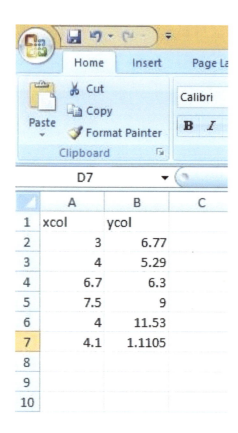

Figure 9: Sample Excel Data to Import

When we click the **Open** button, the Import wizard opens with the data as shown in Figure 10.

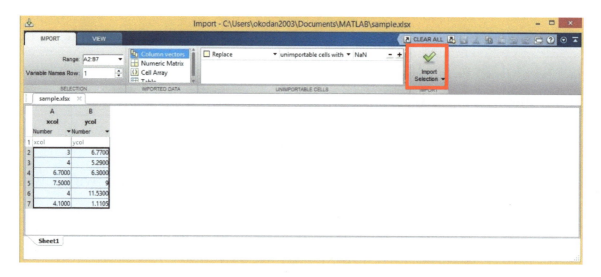

Figure 10: Importing Data (Stage 2)

Next, we click on 'Import Selection' as highlighted in Figure 10. A list drops down, and on this list, we click on **Import Data**, and the data is immediately imported.

Figure 11: Importing Data (Stage 3)

We can verify on the command window that the data has been imported; look in the workspace as shown in Figure 12. Variables named **xcol** and **ycol** have been generated to respectively represent data in the 2 columns of the imported data.

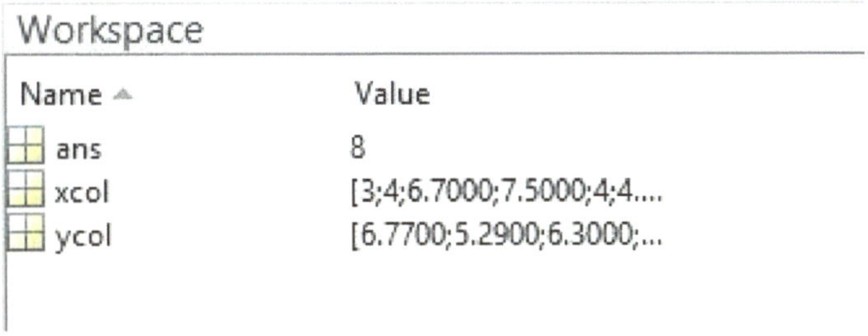

Figure 12: Imported Data shown on the Workspace

You may be itching to see what next we can do with these data after the import. This will be treated in other series of this book. For now, we are just interested to know that you can import data into MATLAB. It's a big step in the learning!

Feel free to play around with the Import Wizard. You can also use it to import data from other file formats (e.g. text files and other spreadsheets).

HINT: Interestingly, there are several other ways we can use MATLAB codes to automatically import external file contents into MATLAB without necessarily going through the Import Wizard, we'll treat these in another series on File Processing.

2.3 Generating Matrices using MATLAB in-built Functions

This is going to be interesting! It's actually like we are just going to begin real programming on MATLAB. So, I'm just going to quickly take out time and explain this:

MATLAB already has lots and lots of in-built functions which make programming with it a lot easier. A function is an already written program that can be used (and re-used) to execute a specific kind of task.

Inputs are usually supplied to the function, and in return, the function produces outputs which depend on the inputs.

The explanation above may not make practical sense if we don't illustrate with one function. Let's start with this one: the MATLAB function called 'zeros'.

2.3.1 zeros

The function 'zeros' is used to create an array of all zeros.

zeros(n) creates an n-by-n array of zeros; this means that if you type **zeros(4)** on the command window, it will give you a 4-by-4 matrix with every entry = 0 as shown below.

$$\text{Zeros}(4) = \begin{matrix} 0 & 0 & 0 & 0 \\ 0 & 0 & 0 & 0 \\ 0 & 0 & 0 & 0 \\ 0 & 0 & 0 & 0 \end{matrix}$$

The 4-by-4 matrix produced is termed a square matrix since the dimensions are equal; it has an equal number of rows as columns.

On the other hand, if what we want is a rectangular array (say, a 3-by-5 array), then the syntax is:

zeros(m,n) which gives an m-by-n array of all zeros. E.g. a 3-by-5 array of zeros can be produced with the code **zeros(3,5)**.

HINT: By the time you get used to these stuff, feel free to advance your understanding of any MATLAB function by going to: Help >> Documentation, on the MATLAB Home Menu, and then searching for the function name in the window that opens.

This is a fantastic way to learn about MATLAB functions because on the same page, you can learn about similar other functions you never knew existed, and perhaps about functions that are newly added to MATLAB. MATLAB is recently being updated twice every year, so you may never know it all.

2.3.2 ones

The function 'ones' is used to create an array of all ones. In a pattern similar to zeros, **ones(n)** creates an n-by-n array of ones, while **ones(m,n)** creates an m-by-n array of all ones. For example, to create a 4-by-6 array of ones, we type **ones(4,6)** on the command window.

$$
\text{ones}(4,6) = \begin{matrix} 1 & 1 & 1 & 1 & 1 & 1 \\ 1 & 1 & 1 & 1 & 1 & 1 \\ 1 & 1 & 1 & 1 & 1 & 1 \\ 1 & 1 & 1 & 1 & 1 & 1 \end{matrix}
$$

2.3.3 eye

The function 'eye' is used to create identity matrices. Similar to ones and zeros, eye(n) creates an n-by-n identity matrix (that is, a matrix of ones on the leading diagonal and zeros everywhere else).

E.g. to create a 5-by-5 identity matrix, we use **eye(5)**.

$$eye(5) = \begin{matrix} 1 & 0 & 0 & 0 & 0 \\ 0 & 1 & 0 & 0 & 0 \\ 0 & 0 & 1 & 0 & 0 \\ 0 & 0 & 0 & 1 & 0 \\ 0 & 0 & 0 & 0 & 1 \end{matrix}$$

Can you tell what **eye(4,5)** will give? See below.

$$eye(4,5) = \begin{matrix} 1 & 0 & 0 & 0 & 0 \\ 0 & 1 & 0 & 0 & 0 \\ 0 & 0 & 1 & 0 & 0 \\ 0 & 0 & 0 & 1 & 0 \end{matrix}$$

2.3.4 rand

The function 'rand' is used to generate uniformly distributed random numbers.

rand(n,m) generates an n-by-m array of random numbers usually in the range between 0 and 1.

For example, **rand(4,3)** gives a 4-by-3 array of random numbers as shown below.

$$rand(4,3) = \begin{matrix} 0.8147 & 0.6324 & 0.9575 \\ 0.9058 & 0.0975 & 0.9649 \\ 0.1270 & 0.2785 & 0.1576 \\ 0.9134 & 0.5469 & 0.9706 \end{matrix}$$

NOTE: The rand function generates different set of random numbers when ran for different times. If for instance we run 'rand(4,3)' again we'll get a set of 4-by-3 array of random numbers different from the set above.

2.3.5 The colon operator (:)

The colon operator is used to generate sequentially arranged series of numbers.

For example, 2:7 generates the sequence of whole numbers from 2 to 8 as below.

2:7 = 2 3 4 5 6 7

This kind of array where all the entries are on a single row is called a 'row vector'. On the contrary, if all the entries are on a single column, we call it a 'column vector'.

The row vector above can be transformed into a column vector using the transpose operator discussed next.

We can also indicate a step size (or increment) in the sequence by including a middle term as illustrated below:

4:3:16 generates a sequence from 4 up to 16 in steps of 3. That is:

4:3:16 = 4 7 10 13 16

0:0.5:2 generates the sequence from 0 to 2 in steps of 0.5 as below.

0:0.5:2 = 0.0000 0.5000 1.0000 1.5000 2.0000

And 5:-5:-25 generates the sequence from 5 to -25 in steps of -5

5:-5:-25 = 5 0 -5 -10 -15 -20 -25

So MATLAB, by default, increases the sequence by steps of 1 if we don't include the middle term.

2.3.6 The transpose operator (')

The transpose operator turns the rows of a matrix into columns, and the columns into rows.

Precisely, if M= $\begin{matrix} 2 & -1 & 7 \\ 3 & 0 & 5 \\ 4 & 4 & -6 \\ -8 & 1 & 1 \end{matrix}$

Then M' will turn the rows of M into columns, and its columns into rows as below.

M' = $\begin{matrix} 2 & 3 & 4 & -8 \\ -1 & 0 & 4 & 1 \\ 7 & 5 & -6 & 1 \end{matrix}$

And so if we have a row vector (let's say a=2:7), then we can transpose it into a column vector using a' as below.

a' = $\begin{matrix} 2 \\ 3 \\ 4 \\ 5 \\ 6 \\ 7 \end{matrix}$

2.3.7 Concatenating matrices

In MATLAB, we can also concatenate (or join) matrices. Supposing we have three matrices a, b and c as these:

a = $\begin{matrix} 2 & -1 & 7 \\ 3 & 0 & 5 \end{matrix}$ b = $\begin{matrix} 5 & 1 \\ -3 & 7 \end{matrix}$ and   c = $\begin{matrix} 3 & -2 & 4 \\ 8 & 19 & -6 \\ 4 & 5 & 6 \\ 4 & 0 & 56 \end{matrix}$

Then we can join a and b side-by-side using [a b] as illustrated below. Observe that we use a space between a and b.

$$[a\ b] = \begin{matrix} 2 & -1 & 7 & 5 & 1 \\ 3 & 0 & 5 & -3 & 7 \end{matrix}$$

This is called horizontal concatenation and can also be exactly achieved using a function called 'horzcat' on MATLAB. To do this, we just use horzcat(a,b) as shown below.

$$horzcat(a,b) = \begin{matrix} 2 & -1 & 7 & 5 & 1 \\ 3 & 0 & 5 & -3 & 7 \end{matrix}$$

We can also join a and c top-by-bottom in MATLAB using [a;c]. Observe here that we use a semicolon between a and c.

$$[a;c] = \begin{matrix} 2 & -1 & 7 \\ 3 & 0 & 5 \\ 3 & -2 & 4 \\ 8 & 19 & -6 \\ 4 & 5 & 6 \\ 4 & 0 & 56 \end{matrix}$$

This is called vertical concatenation and we can also achieve exactly the same thing on MATLAB using the vertcat function. That is, 'vertcat(a,c)' as below.

$$vertcat(a,c) = \begin{matrix} 2 & -1 & 7 \\ 3 & 0 & 5 \\ 3 & -2 & 4 \\ 8 & 19 & -6 \\ 4 & 5 & 6 \\ 4 & 0 & 56 \end{matrix}$$

NOTE: We can only concatenate matrices horizontally if they each have the same number of rows, and vertically if they each have the same number of columns.

We cannot therefore concatenate a and c horizontally because they don't each have the same number of rows. Similarly we cannot concatenate a and b vertically because they don't each have the same number of columns.

Chapter 3

MATLAB OPERATIONS

Here, we want to concentrate on the way in which arithmetic operations like addition, subtraction, multiplication, division, etc are done on MATLAB.

3.1 Addition (+)

We can add two matrices (say, a and b) together if their sizes are the same using the syntax a+b. MATLAB actually adds the elements of matrix, a, to corresponding elements of matrix, b, as illustrated below.

Matrices a and b have to be of the same size.

$$a = \begin{matrix} 3 & -2 \\ 1 & 0 \end{matrix} \qquad \text{and} \qquad b = \begin{matrix} 2 & 1 \\ -3 & 5 \end{matrix}$$

We will be using these same values of a and b all through this chapter. So take note!

$$a + b = \begin{matrix} 5 & -1 \\ -2 & 5 \end{matrix}$$

We can also add a scalar (e.g 5) to a matrix (let's say, a) using the syntax; a+5, and what MATLAB does is to add the value, 5, to each element of matrix, a, as below.

$$a + 5 = \begin{matrix} 8 & 3 \\ 6 & 5 \end{matrix}$$

3.2 Subtraction (-)

We can also perform subtraction on matrices in a way similar to addition. Let's say we want to subtract matrix, b, from matrix, a. That is, a-b. MATLAB subtracts the elements of matrix, b, from corresponding elements of matrix, a. (Illustration below). Matrices a and b also have to be of the same size.

$$a - b = \begin{matrix} 1 & -3 \\ 4 & -5 \end{matrix}$$

And we can also subtract a scalar (e.g. 2) from a matrix (let's say, a) as illustrated below. What MATLAB does is to subtract 2 from each of the elements of matrix, a. The command is a-2.

$$a - 2 = \begin{matrix} 1 & -4 \\ -1 & -2 \end{matrix}$$

3.3 Multiplication (*)

We can also multiply matrices. Here we got to be a bit careful!

There are 2 types of multiplication we can do on MATLAB depending on what we want to achieve; matrix multiplication and array multiplication.

3.3.1 Matrix Multiplication (*)

In matrix multiplication, the matrices to be multiplied are actually treated as matrices. Let's say we want to multiply matrices a and b. The command is: a*b, and the results are as shown below.

$$a * b = \begin{matrix} 12 & -7 \\ 2 & 1 \end{matrix}$$

We do not intend to illustrate how to multiply matrices here, but just to mention this. Matrix multiplication should be very clear to anyone that has taken a course on matrices before. If, however, you have never taken a course on matrices, then you do not need to bother. You can skip this part, and move on to section 3.3.2 on Array Multiplication.

Just before we move on, it's important to remind us that we can only perform matrix multiplication on two matrices if their inner dimensions agree. What does that mean?

If we have

Matrix A   Matrix B
dimension: 3-by-2   dimension: 2-by-3

The inner matrix dimensions here agree since they are both 2,
and so they can be matrix multiplied!

Another illustration:

Matrix A Matrix B
dimension: 3-by-2 dimension: 3-by-2

The inner matrix dimensions here don't agree (they are 2 and 3), and so they cannot be matrix multiplied!

Also, matrix multiplication is not commutative. That is to say, a*b is not the same thing as b*a, watch it!

3.3.2 Array Multiplication (.*)

Array multiplication is more straight-forward! This is the kind of multiplication we are all probably used to. Suppose we want to array multiply 2 matrices (a and b), what MATLAB does is to simply multiply the elements of matrix a with corresponding elements in b (see below). The matrices here therefore have to be of the same size.

The command is a.*b

Observe the dot before the multiplication symbol (*), that is what makes array multiplication different from matrix multiplication: So, a*b means the matrix multiplication of a and b, while a.*b means their array multiplication.

If we use matrices a and b as earlier defined, then their array multiplication gives:

$$a \cdot * \, b = \begin{matrix} 6 & -2 \\ -3 & 0 \end{matrix}$$

Array multiplication is commutative since a.*b gives the same result as b.*a.

WARNING: It has happened a lot of times that someone needs to perform array multiplication, and he/she forgets to put the dot. The program in that case implements matrix multiplication, and either returns an error if the matrices don't conform for matrix multiplication, or runs successfully and gives the wrong (or

unintended) result. So be careful!

Finally, we can also multiply a matrix (let's say, a) with a scalar (say, 4). The command is a*4. What MATLAB does here is to multiply each of the elements in matrix, a, with the number, 4.

$$a * 4 = \begin{matrix} 12 & -8 \\ 4 & 0 \end{matrix}$$

3.4 Division

In a manner that is exactly similar to the matrix and array multiplications, we also have the matrix division (/) and the array division (./).

The matrix division (a/b) is the matrix multiplication of matrix, a, with the inverse of matrix, b. And as earlier advised, this should be of interest only to those that have worked with, and have something to do with, matrices.

$$a/b = \begin{matrix} 0.6923 & -0.5385 \\ 0.3846 & -0.0769 \end{matrix}$$

On the other hand, the array division of matrix, a, by matrix, b, (a./b) is the division of elements of matrix, a, by corresponding elements of matrix, b.

$$a./b = \begin{matrix} 1.5000 & -2.0000 \\ -0.3333 & 0 \end{matrix}$$

And finally, we can divide a matrix (still say, a) with a scalar (say, 3). The command is a/3, and what MATLAB does is to divide each of the elements of matrix, a, with the number, 3.

$$a/3 = \begin{matrix} 1.0000 & -0.6667 \\ 0.3333 & 0 \end{matrix}$$

3.5 Powers (^)

We also have matrix powers and array powers.

For matrix powers, we can raise a matrix (let's say, a) to the power of a scalar (let's say, 3). The command is a^3, and what it means is the matrix, a, multiplied by itself, and multiplied by itself again. That is same as a*a*a as carried out using matrix multiplication.

$$a\textasciicircum 3 = \begin{matrix} 15 & -14 \\ 7 & -6 \end{matrix}$$

For array powers, the command is a.^3, and it simply means each of the elements of matrix, a, raised to power 3.

$$a.\textasciicircum 3 = \begin{matrix} 27 & -8 \\ 1 & 0 \end{matrix}$$

There is also a case where we can raise a matrix (say, a) to an array power of another matrix (say, b). The command is a.^b, and what MATLAB does here is to raise the elements of matrix, a, to corresponding elements in matrix, b.

$$a.\char`\^b = \begin{matrix} 9 & -2 \\ 1 & 0 \end{matrix}$$

And just in case you are contemplating on raising matrix, a, to the matrix power of another matrix b (that is, a^b), I think you should first think of what that would mean! And just in case it means something to you, you may want to contact the MATLAB team. For now, the MATLAB software does not support doing that!

Nice! Nice!! Nice!!! If you made it to this point, then you are good to go! It now becomes easy to follow more in dept lectures or books on various projects. Our ideas in subsequent books are to use real life projects to further teach how to use the MATLAB software. Before you go for other books, try to measure your understanding of what is treated on this book by solving the exercises that follow. We wish you good time with the exercises!

Exercises

1. You wish to enter the given matrix $M = \begin{matrix} 4 & -570 & 1 \\ -1 & 12 & 0 \\ 7 & -9 & 5 \end{matrix}$ into MATLAB, how will you type this at the command prompt?

A. M=[4 -570 1; -1 12 0; 7 -9 5]

B. M=[4; -570; 1; -1; 12; 0; 7; -9; 5]

C. M=[4; -570; 1 -1; 12; 0 7; -9; 5]

D. M=[4 -570 1 -1 12 0 7 -9 5]

2. A matrix is entered as X = [-2 4 5; 19 -6 9; 5 7 20; 0 -70 9] on the MATLAB command window. What is the size of X?

A. 3-by-4   B. 4-by-3   C. 12-by-4   D. 12-by-3

3. The following are TRUE except

A. The command 'zeros(6)' does the same thing as 'zeros(6,6)'

B. 'zeros(3,4)+1' will give the same result as 'ones(3,4)'

C. 'ones(8,1)' is a column vector

D. 'ones(5,4)' will give the same result as 'ones(5)*4'

4. The following commands will generate the matrix A below EXCEPT

$$A = \begin{matrix} 5 & 5 & 5 \\ 5 & 5 & 5 \\ 5 & 5 & 5 \end{matrix}$$

A. A=ones(3)*5   B. A=zeros(3)+5

C. A=(ones(3)*5)'   D. A=ones(3,5)

5. Which of the following will correctly generate the sequence of all even numbers from 20 to 30?

A. 20:30

B. 20:30:2

C. 20:2:30

D. 20:22:30

6. The matrix illustrated below could be correctly generated by which of the following commands?

```
1   4
2   4
3   4
4   4
5   4
6   4
```

A. [ones(1,6) ones(4)]   B. [(1:6)' ones(6,1)*4]

C. [(1:6) ones(4,1)]   D. [(1:6)'; ones(6,1)*4]

7. If matrix A is a 10-by-3 matrix and B is a 10-by-5 matrix, which of the following will NOT return an error on MATLAB?

A. [A; B]   B. [A B]   C. [B; A]   D. A+B

Use matrices a, b, and c described below to answer questions 8 to 10.

$$a = \begin{matrix} 2 & -1 & 7 \\ 3 & 0 & 5 \end{matrix} \qquad b = \begin{matrix} 5 & 1 \\ -3 & 7 \end{matrix} \qquad c = \begin{matrix} 3 & 8 & 1 \\ -1 & 0 & 4 \end{matrix}$$

8. Which of the following commands will return an error on MATLAB?

A. a+b   B. a+c   C. c-a   D. a-c

9. Why would the command 'b-c' return an error on MATLAB?

A. Because the number of rows in b is equal to the number of rows in c

B. Because the size of b is not the same as that of c

C. Because the number of rows in b is not same as the number of columns in c

D. Because there must be errors for first time programmers

10. *(Only for persons conversant with matrices)

The following are CORRECT except

A. b*c will not return an error, but b.*c will

B. a.*c will not return an error, but a*c will

C. a*c will not return an error

D. a.*c will give the same result as c.*a

Answers

1. A

2. B

3. D

4. D

5. C

6. B

7. B

8. A

9. D

10. C